spot

MIGHTY MACHINES

MOTORCYCLES

by Wendy Strobel Dieker

AMICUS | AMICUS INK

engine

throttle

Look for these words and pictures as you read.

sidecar

kickstand

Vroom! Vroom!

Here comes a motorcycle.

A biker rides to work.
She puts on a helmet.
It keeps her safe.

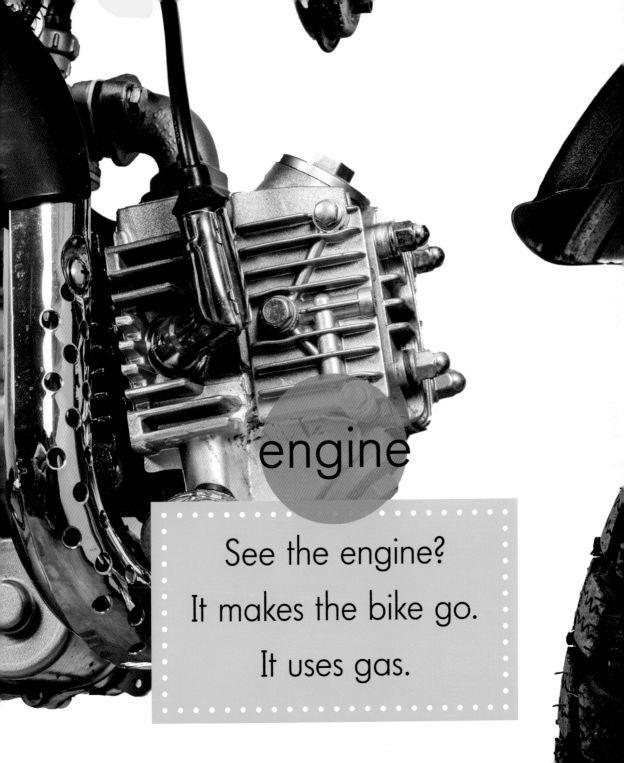

engine

See the engine?
It makes the bike go.
It uses gas.

throttle

See the throttle?

The driver twists it.

This makes the bike go faster.

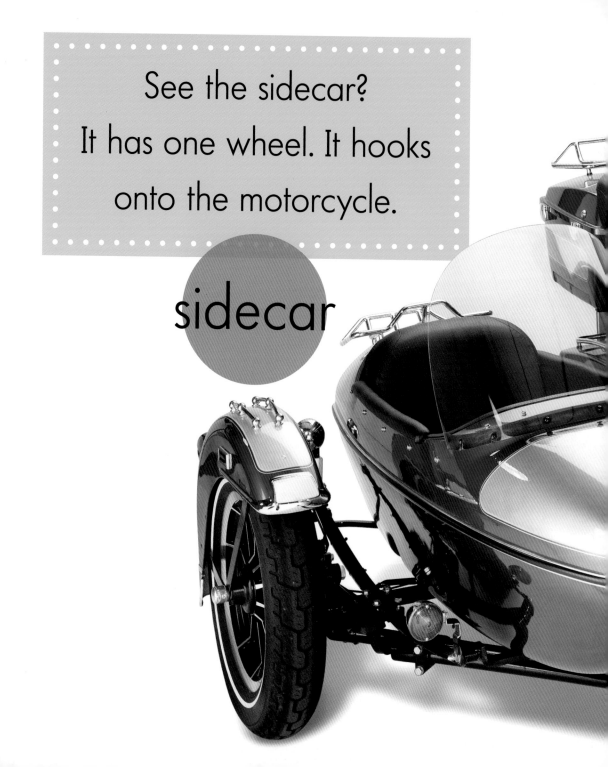

See the sidecar?
It has one wheel. It hooks
onto the motorcycle.

sidecar

See the kickstand?
It holds up the bike.

kickstand

It's time for a ride.

Let's go!

engine

throttle

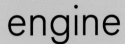

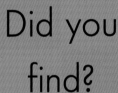

Did you find?

sidecar

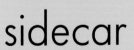

kickstand

Spot is published by Amicus and Amicus Ink
P.O. Box 1329, Mankato, MN 56002
www.amicuspublishing.us

Library of Congress Cataloging-in-Publication Data
Names: Dieker, Wendy Strobel, author.
Title: Motorcycles / by Wendy Strobel Dieker.
Description: Mankato, Minnesota : Amicus, [2020] |
Series: Spot. Mighty machines | Audience: K to grade 3.
Identifiers: LCCN 2018024623 (print) | LCCN
 2018028771 (ebook) | ISBN 9781681517285 (pdf) |
ISBN 9781681516462 (library binding) | ISBN
 9781681524320 (pbk.)
Subjects: LCSH: Motorcycles--Juvenile literature.
Classification: LCC TL440.15 (ebook) | LCC TL440.15 .D54
 2020 (print) | DDC 629.227/5--dc23
LC record available at https://lccn.loc.gov/2018024623

Printed in China

HC   10 9 8 7 6 5 4 3 2 1
PB   10 9 8 7 6 5 4 3 2 1

Alissa Thielges, editor
Deb Miner, series designer
Aubrey Harper, book designer
Holly Young, photo researcher

Photos by Shutterstock/Dimitris
Leonidas cover, 16; iStock/Rawpixel
1; Shutterstock/Jag_cz 3; iStock/
Vesnaandjic 4–5; Getty/Björn Forenius
6–7; iStock/imamember 8–9; Alamy/
Fotografie 10–11; Getty/Henn
Photography 12–13; Shutterstock/Lukas
Gojda 14–15

MOTORCYCLES